STAY FIT

Build a Strong Body

Catherine Reef

TWENTY-FIRST CENTURY BOOKS
A DIVISION OF HENRY HOLT AND COMPANY • NEW YORK

Twenty-First Century Books
A Division of Henry Holt and Company, Inc.
115 West 18th Street
New York, NY 10011

Henry Holt ® and colophon are registered trademarks of
Henry Holt and Company, Inc.
Publishers since 1866

Library of Congress Cataloging-in-Publication Data
Reef, Catherine.
Stay fit: build a strong body / Catherine Reef. — 1st ed.
p. cm. — (Good health guidelines)
Includes index.
Summary: Describes the benefits of exercise and discusses how to
develop a personal fitness program.
1. Physical fitness for children—Juvenile literature. [1. Physical fitness. 2. Exercise.] I. Title. II. Series.
RJ133.R44 1993
613.7—dc20   93-19349 CIP AC

ISBN 0-8050-2441-7
First Edition 1993

Printed in the United States of America
All first editions are printed on acid-free paper ∞ .

10 9 8 7 6 5 4 3 2 1

Photo Credits
Cover: ©Will McIntyre / Photo Researchers
p. 4: ©Richard Hutchings / Photo Researchers; p. 10: ©Dan Burns / Monkmeyer
Press; p. 18: ©Will and Deni McIntyre / Photo Researchers; p. 28: ©Myrleen Fergu-
son / PhotoEdit; p. 36: ©Jack Fields / Photo Researchers; p. 42: ©Daniel Zirinsky /
Photo Researchers; p. 50: ©Chuck Keeler / Tony Stone Images.

Contents

Busy feet tap out quick rhythms in a neighborhood contest of Double Dutch.

1

It's Time to Get Fit!

Listen to the sounds of spring. A basketball bounces—slap, slap, slap—as it is dribbled across a city playground. A bat strikes a baseball. Thwack! Busy feet tap out quick rhythms in a neighborhood contest of Double Dutch. Players shout to one another as they chase a soccer ball across a grassy field.

These are the sounds of active young people who have been lured outdoors by sunshine and warm breezes. In cities, suburbs, and small towns, they are having fun and staying fit.

"I like to ride my bike and run around sometimes," says Diego, who is thirteen.

Ten-year-old J.K. enjoys basketball, "because it's challenging, and it's fun."

"I like to swim," says Roshni, age twelve. "I'm on a swim team."

"I like to ride my bike, play badminton, throw a football around, and go hiking," lists John, thirteen. These activities, says John, are "fun, just fun."

Ashish is ten. He runs, swims, and plays soccer. At fourteen, Nate plays volleyball and basketball. Kelly, twelve, prefers gymnastics. Thirteen-year-old Andrew enjoys floor hockey, "when I get a chance to play it."

Like young people everywhere, these boys and girls care about their health. As they demonstrate, there are many ways to get the exercise that builds a healthy body.

Being in shape does not mean having huge muscles or superhuman strength. A person in top condition may not be a star athlete. Still, he or she is able to enjoy the activities of a full, busy life.

"If you are not active and fit, you get lazy," says Nate. "Your muscles don't get worked. You lose strength. You lose energy." A person in good physical shape, in contrast, has enough strength and energy to do well at schoolwork, sports, and chores around the house—with plenty left over for games and fun.

A physically fit person has a strong heart and lungs that can provide plenty of oxygen to all parts of the body. He or she has strong, firm muscles, just the right amount of body fat, and flexible joints. Being in shape helps people feel confident, alert, and in control.

Many doctors and other health professionals now say that good health involves more than being free of illness or injury. It includes making the most of your body and mind. So to be truly healthy, a person must be physically fit.

Staying in top form means leading an active life—and getting regular exercise. Yet research has uncovered an alarming fact. Too many children do not get enough exercise. Children in the 1990s are less fit than children were in the 1960s.

Researchers have found, for example, that many of today's young people cannot perform simple physical tasks. Half of the girls studied and one-third of the boys could not run a mile in less than ten minutes. They could not do a pull-up. Only a third of those age six to seventeen passed the tests for a strong heart and lungs, flexible joints, a firm abdomen, and a sturdy upper body.

Young people have been gaining weight as well. One study found that since the 1960s, obesity—being 20 percent or more above recommended weight—has increased 54 percent in the six-to-eleven age group and 39 percent in those age twelve to seventeen. Having too much body fat results from poor food choices and inactivity. It can lead to health problems in adult life.

Fitness experts also have expressed concern that most children get too little physical education in school. Although experts recommend daily physical education classes, only one-third of students in American and Canadian schools have "P.E." every day. Just one state, Illinois, requires daily instruction in physical education.

"We see a growing focus on the three Rs," says Dr. Richard Lauzon of the Heart and Stroke Foundation of Canada. "That's all well and good, but people should remember that recreation is an R as well."

Things are different in a number of other countries. Roshni's mother grew up in India. She was required to take part in daily activities after school. "You could not go home," Roshni's mom recalls. "You had to be on the grounds for football, hockey, or whatever they were doing."

Arnold Schwarzenegger, star of *Kindergarten Cop* and other popular films, attended school in Austria. There, says Schwarzenegger, "Everyone who went to school had to do one hour a day of exercise. In addition to that, three times a week, we had sports programs for those who wanted to be competitive—swimming, soccer, basketball, track and field, etc."

Schwarzenegger has served as chairman of the President's Council on Physical Fitness and Sports. Through his writing and personal appearances, he informs students and teachers about the benefits of exercise.

Better school programs would help many youngsters get in shape. But too little physical education is not the only problem. Students' habits outside of school also tend to make them unfit. A young person today is more likely to ride in a car than walk to school or a friend's house. Many boys and girls would rather sit still to watch television or play an electronic game than take part in a sport or play outdoors.

When parents work, their sons and daughters sometimes have trouble finding time for exercise. "They don't let their children do anything while they're gone," observes Andrew. "Then when they get home, it's dark."

Children are often busy, too, with studies, activities, and household chores. "It's hard," says Diego, "because there's lots of homework, and I take piano lessons."

Young people who are out of shape miss a great deal of enjoyment in life. They fail to do the best that they could at home or at school. And those who get too little exercise to strengthen their hearts and lungs may be at risk for heart disease in later life.

"Make no mistake about it," Arnold Schwarzenegger cautions. "The fitness of American youth is a problem."

Every girl and boy can build a strong, flexible body through exercise. Until age seven, it's enough simply to play actively every day. By age eight, children are ready to plan and follow a fitness program—one that provides the different kinds of exercise that they need.

During exercise, several body systems work together. People who work out use their muscles, bones and joints, lungs, heart, and blood vessels. A comprehensive exercise program benefits all of those systems. Exercise increases flexibility—the ability to move muscles and joints through their full range of motion. It improves strength—the amount of force muscles can exert to lift, push, or pull. It also builds endurance—the power to exercise steadily for a long period.

As active young people shoot baskets, climb playground equipment, turn somersaults, and run races, they are building strength, endurance, and flexibility. As they swim laps or speed along on their bikes, they are exercising their hearts and lungs.

They have an important message for boys and girls everywhere: Get busy, and get in shape. "Don't sit around the house all day," advises Diego.

"Be more active," adds Nate. "As my mom says, you're only a kid once."

When a person gets vigorous exercise... the heart and lungs get exercise as well.

2

Muscles, Heart, and Lungs

On a bright and breezy Thursday afternoon, John straps a helmet on his head. He swings a leg over his bicycle and heads for a nearby park, a place that is free from the noise and hazards of traffic. "It feels good to ride," John says. "I do a couple of miles each time I go for a bike ride."

As John rides, the muscles in his legs contract. His feet push down on the pedals, and the bicycle moves forward. The muscles are the body parts that enable a person to move. "The thing you feel working the most is your leg muscles," John observes.

Just like a car or other piece of machinery, muscles need energy if they are to work. A car gets its energy by burning the gasoline stored in its fuel tank. Muscles get their energy by breaking down glycogen, a substance stored within the muscle tissue. The muscles can also draw on the body's stores of fat for energy.

To use glycogen and fat, the muscles require oxygen, which comes from the air. As John draws in a breath, air passes through his nose and down his trachea, or windpipe. The air fills two large organs in his chest—his lungs. The air makes its way into the lungs' many tiny sacs called alveoli. Oxygen from the air passes through the thin walls of the alveoli and enters the bloodstream.

The blood is the body's great transportation system. Traveling through blood vessels called arteries, it carries oxygen from the air and nutrients from food to every cell in the body. The blood uses another group of vessels—the veins—to carry away waste products, such as the carbon dioxide that is produced when the muscles burn glycogen. The carbon dioxide leaves John's body through his lungs when he exhales, or breathes out.

One muscle does the crucial job of moving the blood through the arteries and veins. That muscle is the heart. Every minute of every day, this fist-sized muscle located in the chest beats steadily, pumping the blood through the body.

The heart is divided into four sections, called chambers. Oxygen-rich blood from the lungs enters the chamber called the left atrium. It is then drawn into another chamber, the left ventricle. When the heart contracts, it pushes this blood into the aorta, the body's main artery.

The veins return blood carrying waste products to the chamber known as the right atrium. When the right atrium and right ventricle contract, they squeeze the blood into the pulmonary artery, which carries it back to the lungs.

As John's muscles work harder, they need more and more fuel. His body uses oxygen at a faster rate. His breathing quickens, and his heart beats more rapidly. "You breathe deeper, but still regular," he observes. "You feel your heart beating only if you concentrate on it."

When a person gets vigorous exercise, more than the muscles get a workout. The heart and lungs get exercise as well. Exercise that causes the body to use lots of oxygen is called aerobic. It helps the heart and lungs work well and grow strong.

Biking and swimming are great ways to get aerobic exercise. Rapid walking, jogging, running, jumping rope, and cross-country skiing can all be aerobic, too. In all of these activities, the person exercises without stopping and maintains a steady pace. Chasing and kicking a soccer ball can be aerobic if the action is constant and steady. The same is true for dribbling and shooting baskets. A sport such as baseball is not aerobic, though, because the players spend most of their time standing still.

The heart and lungs get the most benefit from a regular schedule of aerobic exercise. Fitness experts advise people to do three 30-minute aerobic workouts each week.

What's the best activity to choose? Something you like, of course! Choosing an activity that you enjoy helps you stick with your fitness program. It's also possible to vary your activity from one workout to the next in order to keep exercise interesting and fun. If you want to work out with friends or your family, choose a form of aerobic exercise that everyone enjoys. Friends can have fun and gain aerobic benefits from a fast, informal basketball game or a round of Double Dutch. Family members can share a good time during an evening swim at an indoor pool. They can hike together in the woods or a city park.

Some people must consider physical disabilities when deciding how to exercise. Perhaps they have lost the use of one or more limbs or have impaired vision. Although doctors may advise those with severe spinal-cord injuries not to raise their heart rates, most persons with disabilities can benefit from aerobic exercise.

Disabled young people and adults have enjoyed swimming, canoeing, and aerobics for the upper body. Some athletes race or play basketball in lightweight sports wheelchairs. Others have learned to run or ski on artificial limbs. A blind person can go cycling on a tandem, or bicycle built for two.

At the height of aerobic exercise, your heart, lungs, and muscles will be working hard—much harder than when you are standing still. The body needs to start exercising slowly and reach that high level of functioning gradually. For this reason, it's best to begin each workout with a five-minute "warm-up." Activities such as jumping jacks, walking, and slow jogging get the muscles, heart, and lungs warmed up and ready for action. Stretching lowers the risk of certain injuries, such as pulled muscles.

Once you have warmed up well, you are ready to begin twenty to thirty minutes of aerobic activity. How hard should you exercise? That depends on your age and how fit you already are. It's important to exercise at a level that's right for you—and not to try keeping up with someone else.

For example, Kelly might want to begin a walking program with twenty minutes of brisk walking three times a week. She might even alternate periods of walking and jogging. But her sister, Lindsey, is younger and has muscles that are less developed. Lindsey could start with fifteen minutes of brisk walking, three times a week.

As their fitness improved in the weeks ahead, both girls could make their exercise programs more challenging. They could walk for longer periods. They could do a little more jogging. They could also change their route so that some of their walk was uphill, which would make their bodies work harder.

If Diego were to start a bicycling program, he might plan to ride for about thirty minutes at first and to cover a distance of four miles. His sister Andrea, like Lindsey, is in the third grade. She might want to start out biking for twenty-five minutes and cover three miles. Both Diego and Andrea could gradually add to their exercise time and distance as they grew more fit.

If you try to do too much too soon, you will quickly get tired. You will fail to keep up a steady pace. And you will likely end up with sore muscles. Remember, it can take six weeks to become physically fit.

A good way to find out if you are exercising at the right level is to take the "talk test." Even though you may feel that your body is working hard during aerobic exercise, you should be able to talk easily. You may find that you are breathing too hard to talk. If so, you need to slow down the pace of your exercise.

It's also a good idea to drink plenty of water before and during exercise to keep the body cool and replace fluid that is lost as perspiration. Many people find it works well to drink two 8-ounce glasses of water before they exercise and to make sure that water is available while they are working out.

The last part of every aerobic workout should be five minutes of cooling down to give the heart, lungs, and muscles time to get used to a lower level of activity. Your cool down can include exercising at a slower pace, walking slowly, and stretching gently. This is a time to relax and think about how good it feels to get fit.

John rides his bike past a pond where young children toss bread to ducks and geese. He pedals past a playground, where laughing toddlers swing and slide. As he rides, John does not concentrate on his heart, lungs, and muscles, but on the sights and sounds of life in the park. For him, exercise comes naturally.

Having good flexibility helps people to reach, bend, tumble—and shoot baskets.

3

Stretching and Building Strength

J.K. has come to the school playground to practice his basketball shots. His face wears a look of concentration. Carefully, he aims the ball at the basket that hangs high above. His knees bend slightly, and then he springs upward. His arm reaches out, propelling the ball into the air. "Your arm does stretch a lot," says J.K. about shooting baskets.

The bones in J.K.'s arms and hands, along with the rest of the bones in his body, form his skeleton. The skeleton is the hard structure that supports the body's soft tissues. The bones are too hard and stiff to bend, yet J.K. can crouch, jump, twist, reach, and stretch. All of this motion takes place at the joints, such as the knees, elbows, wrists, and ankles. The joints are the spots where bones come together.

Inside J.K.'s joints, a tough white tissue called cartilage cushions the bones to keep them from rubbing against one another. A liquid called synovial fluid "oils" the joints, so that they move smoothly. Strong bands of tissue known as ligaments keep the bones in place. The ligaments are flexible enough to allow movement but strong enough to hold the bones together.

Stretching the joints keeps them flexible. And having good flexibility helps people to reach, bend, tumble— and shoot baskets. Stretching also keeps the muscles long and supple, so that they, too, have a greater range of motion. And best of all, stretching feels great!

Here are some stretches that help to keep muscles and joints flexible. These exercises stretch the large muscle groups used in many physical activities. They are good to do every day, or as part of warming up or cooling down. Remember that stretching involves gentle movement. It should feel good and should never be forced.

Arm and Hand Stretch

This exercise stretches the muscles and joints from the shoulders to the fingertips.

Raise one arm into the air and stretch it upward, as if you were reaching for a juicy apple growing on a tree. Hold the stretch for ten to thirty seconds. Stretch out the fingers and then relax them. Do this two or three times with each arm and hand.

Arm Circles

Here's another stretch to get the arms limbered up and ready for exercise.

Extend the arms straight out to the sides. Make twenty small circles with the arms. Make twenty more circles that are larger, and twenty more that are larger still.

Shoulder Stretch

This exercise really improves flexibility in the shoulder joint.

While standing, raise the right arm in the air. Then bend the elbow, so that the palm of the hand touches the back between the shoulders. Place the left hand behind the back and reach up, trying to touch the fingers of the right hand. Hold the stretch for ten to thirty seconds. Stretch each shoulder twice in this way.

Lower Back Stretch

In this exercise, moving the legs helps to stretch the muscles in the lower part of the back.

Lie on your back with your legs straight and relaxed. Now, bend the left leg, bringing the knee toward the chest. With both hands, grasp the left leg under the knee. Gently pull the leg toward the left shoulder. Hold the stretch for ten to thirty seconds. Do this twice with each leg.

Wall Stretch

"My dad does this one," Ashish says. Runners such as Ashish's father often do this exercise to stretch the muscles in the calf, the lower part of the leg.

Stand a little more than arm's length from a wall. Put your hands forward and lean against the wall. Extend your right foot backward. Keeping both feet on the floor, lean forward and bend the left knee, so that the stretch is felt in the right calf. Stretch each calf in this way ten times.

Hamstring Stretch

The hamstring is the muscle in the back of the thigh.

Stand in front of a chair seat or other flat surface that is almost waist high. Rest your right foot on the chair. Keeping the right leg straight, bend forward from the hips, feeling the stretch in the back of the thigh. Hold this position for one or two seconds. Stretch the right hamstring ten times. Then repeat the stretches on the left hamstring.

Hip Stretch

This is a great way to stretch the hip joint and the muscles that surround it.

Kneel on your right knee with your left leg bent and in front of you. Place the left foot flat on the floor. Keep your head and shoulders erect, and rest your hands on your left knee. Then, with your left knee and toes pointing straight ahead, press the hips forward and down, so that the left knee bends over the left foot—and not to the side. Do ten hip stretches with the left leg bent and ten with the right leg bent.

Like J.K., Andrea often comes to the playground. She likes to shoot baskets, too, but today she is climbing on the jungle gym. When Andrea hangs from the bars, she depends on her muscles to hold up her weight. She is giving them extra work to do, and she is making them stronger. Does Andrea feel her muscles working hard? "Mm-hmm!" she replies.

The muscles that people use for movement are called striated muscles. Their long cells are sometimes called fibers. When people make their muscles work, the fibers grow thicker and stronger. Strong muscles are able to work and play hard. They help a person lift, climb a rope, or swing a bat.

As Andrea exercises each day, changes take place in her body that improve her endurance. Her muscle cells develop more mitochondria. These are the microscopic parts of the cells that take in oxygen. Her body forms more of the tiny blood vessels called capillaries, to bring an increased supply of oxygen-rich blood to her muscle cells. With greater endurance, Andrea can work or play longer before she gets tired out.

The following exercises build strength and endurance. Each one makes the muscles lift some of the body's weight. As the muscles work harder, they grow stronger. You can build endurance by gradually increasing the number of times each exercise is done.

How many times should you do each strength-building exercise? Kenneth Cooper, M.D., a fitness expert who is the director of the Aerobics Center in Dallas, Texas, explains how you can answer this question. Test yourself, he says, to see how many times you can do the exercise. Divide this total in half to find the amount in a set, or the number of times you should do each exercise at one time.

You may find, after a few weeks of exercising, that doing one set of each exercise has become too easy. When this happens, Dr. Cooper suggests that you work through the sets twice, and then three times in the weeks ahead.

When three sets lose their challenge one day, it's time to test again and determine a new number of exercises in each set. You can then start again with one set of each exercise, then two sets, and then three.

Allow yourself a thirty-second rest period between each set of exercises.

Curl-Up

This exercise targets the muscles of the abdomen.

Lie down with your knees bent and feet flat on the floor. Cross your arms on your chest, and place your hands on your shoulders. Tuck your chin to your chest, and then slowly raise your head, shoulders, and chest. Touch your elbows to your thighs. Then slowly lower yourself to the floor. It may help to have a partner hold your feet.

Push-Up

Push-ups strengthen the muscles in the chest, arms, shoulders, back, and legs.

Keeping your body straight, support your weight with your hands and toes. Your hands should be slightly more than shoulder width apart. Keeping your back straight, slowly lower your body to the floor. Then push back up again.

Modified Push-Up

Boys and girls who can't lift all of their body weight in a regular push-up may wish to keep their knees on the floor. It's still important, though, to keep the back straight. Once their strength increases, these exercisers can move up to doing a full push-up.

Pull-Up

Doing pull-ups helps to strengthen the arms and upper body. Begin by hanging from a bar with the palms of your hands facing away from your body. Pull yourself up until your chin is slightly higher than the bar. Then lower yourself until your arms are straight again.

Tall people may need to bend their knees when doing pull-ups to keep their feet from touching the ground.

Modified Pull-Up

Some people cannot get their chins over a bar because they are not yet strong enough to lift their own body weight. They can strengthen their arms and upper body in another way.

To do a modified pull-up, place a strong pole across the seats of two chairs that are standing four feet apart. Lie on your back between the two chairs and under the bar. With your hands shoulder width apart, grasp the bar. Make sure your palms are facing away from your body. Keeping your body straight, pull yourself up until your chest touches the bar. Then lower yourself to the floor.

When modified pull-ups become easy, it's time to start doing regular pull-ups.

Heel Rise

This exercise strengthens the calves and ankles.

Stand up with your feet shoulder width apart. Slowly raise yourself on your toes, as high as possible. Then lower yourself to the starting position.

Leg Lift

Leg lifts build strong muscles in the outer thighs and hips.

Lie on your left side, supporting your upper body on your left elbow. Place your right hand on the floor in front of you for balance. Keep the left knee slightly bent. Now, slowly raise your right leg as far as you are able, and then lower it to the starting position.

After completing a set lifting the right leg, lie on your right side and do a set lifting your left leg.

Hip Rise

The hip rise strengthens the triceps (the muscles in the back of the arms) as well as the chest muscles.

Sit with your hands on the floor next to your hips. Your hands should be placed palms down, with the fingers pointing away from you. Keeping your arms straight, raise your hips into the air until your body forms a straight line. Only your heels and hands should be on the floor. Then slowly lower yourself to the starting position.

Both the parent and the child must...get involved if the...fitness program is to succeed.

$$\frac{4}{}$$

Your Fitness Program

Ashish's father got interested in exercise as a teenager. He took up field hockey and cycling. "And somehow," he says, "it made a difference as far as my academic work was concerned." As he became fit, his grades improved.

A similar thing happened when Ashish's father started running three years ago. As he explains, "It makes me more alert at work since I started running." He would like to see his children benefit from fitness as he has. And so when Ashish decided to start running last year, his dad says, "I encouraged him." The father and son compete in races, and they practice running on the track of a nearby high school.

Even if they don't take part in an exercise program themselves, adults can support and encourage young people who want to get fit. A parent, grandparent, aunt, uncle, or other caring adult can provide supervision and rides to the pool or practice. Adults can help young people set aside time in their schedule for exercise.

According to Dr. Kenneth Cooper, an adult's help is always needed. "Both the parent and the child must somehow get involved," Dr. Cooper believes, "if the kid fitness program is to succeed."

That's why the first step in planning your fitness program is to talk it over with a parent or other adult. Dr. Cooper and other fitness experts advise young people and adults to work together to draw up a Fitness Contract. This is an agreement, on paper, of what the fitness program will accomplish. Writing down their plans helps people think carefully about how they will get fit. It makes them take the program seriously, so they are more likely to stick with it.

The first thing to list on your Fitness Contract are your fitness goals—the reasons you want to get fit. Good health is often an important reason. Most young people want to do what's best for their health. Physical fitness improves health now and helps to protect health in years to come. Other fitness goals might include improved ability to run or play games, a more attractive appearance, more energy, better performance in school, spending more time with the family, or joining a team and making friends.

Next, the contract lists specific program goals. This is the place to write down what the program will include, in as much detail as possible. One person's program goals might look like this:

• Biking for twenty to thirty minutes, two afternoons a week

- Swimming at an indoor pool one evening each week
- Strength and endurance exercises three times a week after dinner

Another person might take a different approach:

- Join a basketball team—practice on Tuesdays after school, games on Saturday mornings
- Jumping rope or biking with friends after school, two times a week for thirty minutes
- Strength and endurance exercises every other day

Both of these individuals could stretch as part of warming up and cooling down.

Planning also includes thinking ahead about any obstacles that might make it hard for you to reach your fitness goals. A busy schedule can be an obstacle for many people. And working adults cannot always find time to take their children to lessons and practice sessions.

Lack of money can be an obstacle. Kelly, for example, would like to take a dance class, but the family budget won't allow it. Even an activity like watching television could even be an obstacle if a favorite show comes on at the time you had planned to take a walk.

Andrew brings up another concern that keeps some young people from exercising: "You feel like if you do something stupid, someone is going to laugh." Negative thoughts such as this are a common obstacle. Many girls and boys actually talk themselves out of getting fit. By putting themselves down, they miss out on new activities.

Some would-be exercisers get discouraged when they see that others are better athletes than they are. They drop out of sports programs because they think they will never be any good. This is a mistake. Everyone develops at his or her own rate, and everyone can get fit. As young people grow bigger and more mature, they also grow stronger. They gain control over their bodies, and many see their athletic skills improve.

Adolescents often discover, as John did, that they are "late bloomers." They catch up to others in athletic ability—or even pass them by. "I'm getting better at sports now," John says, "and I have developed more of an interest in them."

Once people know their obstacles, they can plan ways around them. They can prevent the obstacles from causing the fitness program to fail. Someone with a favorite TV show could do stretching and strength-building exercises while watching and could schedule a walk or workout for another time. A busy person might set aside specific times for exercise, and even mark them on a calendar.

Working adults, too, may be able to adjust their schedules. Ashish's dad goes to work early on the days when his son has soccer practice so that he can come home in time to take him there. "I'm lucky that I can work flex time," this busy father says. However, he admits that "it's very hard for a lot of parents to do that."

There is even a way to overcome negative self-talk. It's a method called "thought stopping." People who catch themselves thinking a negative thought can tell themselves, "Stop!" Then they can replace the negative thought with a positive one: "I haven't been athletic in the past, but I may be in the future—I could be a late bloomer. Besides, the goal of my fitness program is not to become a star athlete, but to get in shape." They can even imagine themselves succeeding.

And once they do succeed, these exercisers deserve to be rewarded. Psychologists say that rewards reinforce people's actions. Because they like getting the rewards, people repeat the good behavior that earns them those rewards. Looking forward to receiving rewards will inspire you to keep on exercising.

What kinds of rewards should you receive? That depends on your likes and interests. Your reward could be a book or a poster for your room. But it doesn't have to be something that you buy. You could ask for permission to stay up late and watch a movie on the weekend. Perhaps you would like your mom or dad to prepare a special meal. You might ask your grandmother to take you to a museum. Rewards such as these bring people closer and make for happy memories.

You can list the obstacles that you have identified, your strategies for overcoming them, and your rewards on your Fitness Contract. The contract may also spell out what the adult will do to help the fitness program succeed. The following page gives you an example of a Fitness Contract.

A Sample Fitness Contract

Date_____

I agree to follow this program to meet my fitness goals.

My goals are: Better health; be a better runner; have more energy and fun.

Planned Program	Obstacles	Strategies
Take a brisk walk or ride bike 30 min. 3 days a week after school. Strength/endurance exercises 3 days a week after school. Shoot baskets with friends Saturday mornings at school playground. Daily stretching.	Sometimes I'd rather listen to the radio than get out and exercise.	Wear radio with head-phones while walking.

Rewards: If I follow my fitness program all week, I can take a "night off" from doing the dishes on Friday.

_____

(child's signature)

I agree to walk or bike with (child) at least once a week. I will remind (child) to stick with the program. Also, I will do the dishes on Fridays if (child) follows the program all week.

_____

(adult's signature)

Once you complete your own Fitness Contract and start your exercise program, you may need to make some changes. Plans that look good on paper don't always work out smoothly. For example, the young person who wrote this sample contract may find that the plan to shoot baskets every Saturday doesn't work because the family shops for groceries and cleans the house on that day. When something like this happens, it's OK to change the Fitness Contract so that the program will succeed.

Many people like to record their progress in a fitness program, and you may want to do this, too. You might keep track, on a chart or calendar, of how far you bike or walk during each workout. You may also note how many strength-building exercises you complete.

Some young people like to decorate their chart or calendar with stars or stickers when they meet certain fitness goals. Go ahead and decorate yours, too. And be sure to hang this colorful record in a spot where you can see it often. It will be a cheery reminder that you are getting fit.

Team members...are working together to achieve individual goals.

5

Joining a Team

The sky grows dark as evening approaches, and a cool wind starts to blow. But the air is bright and moist and warm at the indoor pool where Roshni is swimming.

Roshni's swim team is holding a practice session. As the boys and girls kick their way across the pool, holding buoyant blue kick boards out in front of them, they strengthen the muscles in their legs. The sound of splashing is everywhere.

"I'm tired," Roshni tells a teammate, but there is little time to rest. The team is ready to practice the backstroke. Before the practice session ends, they will work on three other strokes as well—the butterfly, breaststroke, and freestyle, or crawl. They work to improve their form and speed. "I want to get better each time I swim," Roshni explains.

With all of the members doing their best, the group will score well in meets against other teams. "You have your individual goals, but you also work for your team ranking," says Roshni.

Like Roshni, thousands of girls and boys take part in organized sports, and their numbers are growing rapidly. For example, more than 1.5 million young people played on United States Soccer Federation teams in 1989. Just ten years earlier, those teams had only 100,000 members. In 1990, 638,000 girls belonged to softball teams. In 1980, less than half that many—306,000 girls—played organized softball.

Most beginners are excited when they sign up for a sport. They hope to have a good time and improve their ability. Adults sometimes tell them that the skills they learn on a team will help them in later life. For the majority of young athletes, sports are an enjoyable experience. But others soon get discouraged and quit. They decide that they dislike the sport, and they may avoid team sports for the rest of their lives.

Why do these young people drop out? Often their goals are different from those of the adults in charge. These boys and girls may find themselves on a team that stresses winning and competition. And during meets, the coaches may keep the best players in the competition while other team members watch from the sidelines.

Adults are correct when they say that team sports can teach useful skills. But those skills do not include winning at all costs. According to Pam Ambrose, the program coordinator for Roshni's swim team, belonging to a team can teach young people sportsmanship, cooperation, listening skills, and time management. "They learn to focus and concentrate," Ms. Ambrose says. The team members also gain from knowing one another. "They are working together to achieve individual goals. They spur one another on."

Roshni claims that she benefits from her teammates' cheers and pep talks. "The group helps you," she believes. "They encourage you to do the strokes and do as much as you are supposed to do."

Sports can show young people that satisfaction comes from doing a job well. They can demonstrate how each person's effort helps the group. On occasion, to help players learn these lessons, sports organizations will alter the rules of a game. For example, some leagues have changed baseball rules for young players, so that an inning doesn't end until everyone has had a turn at bat.

Some children drop off a team because they have not reached the level of development that the sport requires. They are unable to play well, and others call them clumsy. Each sport demands certain skills that young people acquire as they mature. Baseball players must be able to follow the ball with their eyes and predict where it will land. Tennis requires good hand-eye coordination—players must keep their eyes on the ball and have their arms ready to swing at it.

Children develop the ability to catch a ball that has been thrown to them at around age five. This is also the age when they can learn to ride a bike. Five-year-olds are not ready, though, to play team sports. Their eyes have not developed enough to follow a baseball. They have a short attention span and so are likely to lose interest in a game.

The ability to follow a ball with the eyes develops by the age of six or seven. Children at this age also see a big improvement in their gymnastics skills—jumping, running, and balancing. But they don't have the coordination needed to hit a ball that has been pitched to them. Emotionally, they may have trouble handling win-lose situations.

Nine- and ten-year-olds can at last hit a ball or shoot a basket. Still, they may lack the attention span needed to endure long practice sessions with a large group of teammates. Most people have all of the skills needed for sports by the time they reach their preteen years.

Choosing an activity that's right for your age and skill level will help to keep sports participation fun and worthwhile. It is also important to choose an activity you enjoy, so that you will want to stick with it. Your city, town, or county recreation department can tell you what kinds of teams are forming in your area. In some communities, the Boys' and Girls' Clubs sponsor a variety of team sports.

You may want to try several sports to find out which ones you like best. And if you get in shape before the season begins, you will have the flexibility, strength, and endurance that your sport requires. When you are ready to join a team, look for one that gives everyone a chance to take part. You are more likely to enjoy a team that values learning and fun and not simply winning.

If you think there is too much pressure to compete and win on your team, tell an adult in your family. He or she can discuss the problem with the other families and the coaches, and a change may be made. If nothing changes, then it's time to find another team—one that helps you reach your goals.

Sports can provide challenge and pleasure to athletes of all ages and skill levels. The champion runner and long jumper Jackie Joyner-Kersee understands this concept well. As a member of the United States Olympic track team, she has faced the stiffest competition in the world. Yet her sport is still a source of delight. "Jumping has always been the thing for me," she says. "It's like leaping for joy."

People who plan an exercise program also must plan for safety.

6

Play It Safe

In February 1991, while he was walking with some friends, Nate started to cross the street. "I wasn't looking," Nate recalls. "My parents say, 'Look both ways.' I didn't listen that day. Three steps into the road, I was hit."

Nate had walked right into the path of a swiftly moving car. The accident left him with a mild concussion—his brain received a slight injury when his head hit the pavement. He suffered a broken thumb and a badly broken knee that needed surgery. The knee still is "not the best," says Nate. "When I bend it, it kind of tightens up."

Nate is using physical therapy to strengthen his leg and improve the use of his knee. Every week, he exercises with weights at the nearby YMCA. When he swims in the YMCA's pool, he works the muscles in his legs and the rest of his body.

No one knows better than Nate that people who plan an exercise program also must plan for safety. Accidents and injuries can occur anywhere—on the road or sidewalk, in the water, on playgrounds and playing fields.

All walkers, runners, and bikers need to be alert for cars and other vehicles, as Nate so painfully learned. Not only have walkers and joggers been struck, but nearly half of all biking accidents involve a motor vehicle. Wearing brightly colored clothing and using reflectors on your bike will make you more visible.

But remember, even with these attention getters, you can't be sure that every motorist sees you. Drivers may find it especially hard to see exercisers when the sun goes down. For this reason, the American Academy of Pediatrics advises children not to ride their bikes at dusk or after dark. It's better to call a parent or other adult who cares for you if you need a ride.

Bicyclers can take some other steps to keep themselves safe. These include riding on the right side of the road, with the flow of traffic. Using hand signals when you plan to turn or stop lets drivers know what you will do. And always stop and look in all directions before entering a street, turning, or crossing any intersection.

Check out your bicycle, too. It's worth a trip to a bicycle repair shop to be sure that the tires, brakes, handlebars, and seat are all in good condition.

A bike that is too large or too small is hard to control, so check that your bike is the right size for you. If you straddle the top bar of a bicycle and keep your feet on the ground, there should be about an inch of space between your crotch and the bar. This measurement can be done only on a boy's bike, but it will help you choose the right size bicycle whether you ride a boy's or girl's bike.

Bikers need one more piece of equipment—an approved safety helmet. A bicycle helmet protects your head from serious injury in case of an accident or fall. It can even save your life. You can be sure a helmet offers good protection if it meets the safety criteria of the American National Standards Institute (ANSI) or the Snell Memorial Foundation. Another way to protect yourself is to observe changes in the road or sidewalk. Riders who are surprised by a patch of gravel, the curb, the shoulder, a drainage grate, or a pothole may lose control of their bicycles. Uneven pavement can cause runners to trip and fall.

Those hazards are under your feet or wheels. Another hazard comes from above. When people exercise outdoors, their skin is exposed to ultraviolet radiation from the sun. These rays can cause sunburn. And over time, they can bring on changes in the skin's cells that may result in cancer. Doctors now diagnose more than 500,000 cases of skin cancer each year, and that number is rising.

The sun's rays are strongest between 11 A.M. and 3 P.M., so it's good to avoid exposure to sunlight during those hours, even on cloudy days. Using a sunscreen helps to protect the skin from ultraviolet rays. A product with a sun protection factor (SPF) of 15 or higher will give adequate protection. This number is printed on the label. A waterproof sunscreen will remain on the skin during swimming. A hat can protect your head from the sun, and light clothing can safeguard other parts of your body.

In Australia, people remind themselves to "slip, slop, and slap." They slip on a shirt, slop on some sunscreen, and slap on a hat. These are particularly good habits for children because people get most of their exposure to the sun by the time they reach the age of eighteen.

Exercisers also need to dress right for their activity—and for the weather. For weight-bearing exercise, such as walking, running, or aerobic dance, it's best to wear sneakers or running shoes that fit properly and support and cushion the feet. Layers of warm clothing work well on cold days. As the body grows heated from activity, some of the layers can be removed. Light, loose clothing is best in warm weather.

But even in light clothing, the body may have trouble controlling its temperature on very hot or humid days. If exercisers fail to take care, their body temperature may rise to a dangerous level. Heavy sweating, nausea, and weakness are signs of a condition called heat exhaustion. They mean that the person needs to stop exercising, move into the shade or an air-conditioned room, and drink liquids.

However, a person who develops hot, dry skin, along with a headache, rapid pulse, faintness, and flushing, may have heat stroke. *This is a medical emergency. The person needs to see a doctor as soon as possible.*

Dr. Kenneth Cooper advises checking the weather report on hot or sticky days. If the temperature in degrees Fahrenheit and the humidity index total 150 or higher, Cooper says, children should not exercise outdoors.

A favorite activity is swimming, which brings boys and girls into a new environment—the water. The first safety rule for swimmers is to learn to swim confidently and well. The YMCA and many community recreation departments offer swimming classes for people of different ages and ability. These organizations frequently provide lessons to the disabled as well.

But even the best swimmers can run into difficulty. That's why it's always wise to swim with other people. Swimmers should also make sure that a lifeguard, parent, or other adult is providing supervision.

Diving presents special concerns. Some divers have received serious injuries to their heads or spines because they collided with the bottom of a pool, an object under the water, or another swimmer while diving. These injuries could be avoided if everyone followed some safety rules.

For example, before diving, it makes sense to determine how deep the water is. Swimmers should always dive into the deep end of a pool and never into the shallow end. They should also make sure that the bottom is free of obstacles and that no one is in the way. Even when diving in familiar water, young people need to remember that they are growing fast. They may have to adjust the depth of their dive.

Sadly, crime is a problem in many cities and suburbs today. For this reason, people in these communities often exercise in pairs or groups. They are less likely to be crime victims when they are with others than when they are alone. Adults often set limits for the children they care for on the places they may go alone or with friends. It's smart for families to go over the guidelines at the start of an exercise program.

Does safe exercise sound like a long list of rules to remember? Many people feel this way when they first decide to get fit. But the rules quickly become good habits—habits that will prevent injuries and help you enjoy a full, active life.

Something as simple as being active can do so much for good health.

7

A Healthy Life

Spring turns into summer, a time for shorts and T-shirts and long, active days with friends. Nate packs his bags to spend a few weeks with his father, who lives in another state. Diego's family plans a trip to the beach.

Lindsey laces up her roller skates while her sister, Kelly, walks to the mall with her friends. "Now that Kelly's older, she gets more freedom to go walking places," says the girls' mother, Barb. But Kelly jokes, "If we had our licenses, we would ride."

Walking, skating, or swimming—these are just ' of the many ways to have fun and be active. Stayin, the move keeps young hearts and lungs strong and working well. Exercise maintains strength, endurance, and flexibility. Many active people also discover that physical fitness improves their health in other ways.

Often, those who exercise take an interest in nutrition. They like to give their active bodies the fuel that they need and to avoid foods that can be harmful to health. "I eat right," says Nate. "I eat vegetables and a well-balanced meal. I drink juice and milk. I eat fish and chicken."

Andrew tells himself, "If you want to snack, snack on something light, something like popcorn, grapes, or raisins."

Food provides energy for all of the day's activities. Foods such as bread, pasta, rice, cereal, and potatoes are rich in carbohydrates, which the body uses to make glycogen. The body uses the energy from carbohydrates quickly and easily. People also get energy from the fats that they eat.

The energy in food is measured in calories. When a person consumes more calories than he or she can use, the extra ones are stored as body fat. This fat is used up only if the body needs more energy than the food has supplied. A gram of carbohydrate supplies four calories of energy. A gram of fat contains nine calories. That's why eating too many high-fat foods can easily add unwanted body fat.

There are two types of fats in food: unsaturated fats and saturated fats. Most vegetable oils, such as olive, peanut, corn, sunflower, and soybean oils, are unsaturated fats. Saturated fat is found mostly in foods from animal sources, such as meat and milk. Two vegetable oils—coconut oil and palm oil—are also saturated fats.

While eating too much fat of any kind provides people with too many calories, saturated fats pose another risk. Over the years, a diet that is high in saturated fats can cause a buildup called plaque to form inside the arteries. This process, which often begins in childhood, can lead to heart disease in later life.

Food gives people more than energy. It supplies the materials the body needs to grow and maintain its tissues. Proteins are the substances used to build and repair cells in the muscles, blood, bones, skin, and other organs. Proteins also provide calories—four calories per gram. Meat, fish, beans, eggs, milk, and other dairy foods are all good sources of protein.

The body also needs very small amounts of the substances called vitamins and minerals. Vitamins play a role in the many chemical reactions that take place within the body. Minerals are used to build bones and teeth. They form part of red blood cells. They maintain the body's fluids, and, like vitamins, they aid in chemical reactions.

The way to be sure that the body gets all of the nourishing substances, or nutrients, that it needs is to eat a variety of foods. The U.S. Department of Agriculture's "food pyramid" can help you choose a healthy diet. It's best to select most of your foods from the groups near the base of the pyramid—breads and cereals, vegetables, and fruit. Use care when choosing from the groups higher up on the pyramid, such as dairy products and meat, fish, and beans. Some items in these groups are high in fat. Fats, oils, and sweets make up the highest group on the pyramid. Foods in this group offer calories but little else.

Those who combine a healthful diet with regular exercise receive another benefit. They are able to control their weight. This is a benefit that Andrew appreciates. "I like to try to lose weight," he readily admits, "because I'm not thin." Exercise is an important part of Andrew's weight-control program. As he explains, "If I didn't take fencing lessons and go swimming, I would be over-weight."

For years, people with too much body fat have gone on a "diet." They have eaten small meals and counted calories in an attempt to lose weight. This method usually has failed. Many dieters felt too hungry for much of the time and could not stick with their plan. Others lost their extra pounds but gained the weight back once they went off of their diets.

When people diet in this way, much of the weight they lose is not fat but water and lean tissue, such as muscle. Their bodies react to dieting as if they were facing starvation, saving stored fat for future energy needs.

Exercise burns calories and so helps people use up their unwanted body fat. That's why weight-loss experts recommend sensible eating—choosing nutritious, low-fat foods—combined with regular exercise to get weight under control.

But before starting a weight-loss program, it's important to find out whether you really need to lose body fat. Many young people, especially girls, who think of themselves as "fat" do not really have a weight problem. As they try to get thinner, they deny themselves needed nutrients, and they place themselves at risk for eating disorders such as anorexia nervosa. In this serious condition, a person diets to the point of causing severe health problems or even death. A nurse or physician can tell you whether your weight is correct for your height and sex. And if a health professional finds that you do need to lose body fat, make sure that a knowledgeable adult supervises your weight-loss program.

Exercise can improve health in another way as well, by reducing stress. Stress is the word that describes the way someone reacts to a threatening situation. The heart beats faster, sending extra blood to the arms and legs. The muscles tense, and hormones—chemicals that stimulate the body to act—flood the system. The person gets ready for "fight or flight," which means he or she is ready to fight against the threat or run away from it.

This reaction worked well thousands of years ago, when people faced such threats as wild animals. But it is a poor way to handle the threats that exist today. Young people experience stress, for example, if they feel looked down upon by their classmates. Family problems, such as divorce, commonly cause stress as well. Moving from one home to another can be stressful, and so can pressure to succeed in sports or in school.

When stress occurs day after day, it takes a toll on health and enjoyment of life. Girls and boys under stress often complain of more stomachaches and headaches than others their age. They may also have more colds and sore throats. Their grades may decline, and they may have behavior problems in school.

Intense stress can lead to a condition called depression. A person with depression feels sad all the time and believes that life has little meaning. In severe cases, depression can result in suicide. *Young people who are depressed need professional help.* A physician, nurse, or school counselor can put a child and his or her family in touch with a qualified therapist. A therapist is someone with years of training in helping people solve their problems. He or she can help ease the depression.

Someone under stress may turn to alcohol or other drugs to relieve the unpleasant feelings. This is a poor way to cope. Drugs cannot ease the problems that the girl or boy faces. But they can harm health and cause the user to become dependent on them.

There are better, healthful ways to ease stress and relax the body and mind. Talking with a parent or other adult may help a young person understand the causes of stress and perhaps find ways to change or avoid them.

Many people relax by having fun with their families and friends. Others like to enjoy a hobby, read a good book, or watch a funny movie. Controlled relaxation exercises can be useful as well. Often explained on cassette tapes, these exercises help clear the mind and relax all of the muscles in the body.

Regular physical activity has been shown to relax muscles, improve mood, and reduce depression. As a boy, the basketball star Julius Erving dealt with the stress of racism, poverty, and family problems on the ball court. "I'd play by myself for hours," Erving recalls, "and when I got through, whatever was bothering me didn't matter any more."

Nate lessens his stress by taking long walks with his mother. They like to stroll along an old canal. "If you had to think about something, you could do it there," he says. "If I have a problem with school or schoolwork, I'll say, 'Mom, let's take a ride up to the canal.' She'll say, 'Sure.' Then we'll take a walk and talk about it."

Spring, summer, fall, or winter, exercise can make you feel good. It can make you look good, too, by giving you a healthy glow and a fit, trim body. Getting fit boosts energy for work and for play. It's exciting to know that something as simple as being active can do so much for good health.

As you grow older, you will make more of the decisions that affect your health. You are moving toward adulthood, a time when you will take over the job of caring for yourself. The good habits you begin now can last a lifetime. The exercise you get today and every day will keep you healthy and doing your best for years to come.

For Further Reading

Bursztyn, Peter G. *Physiology for Sportspeople: A Serious User's Guide to the Body*. New York: Manchester University Press, 1990.

Cooper, Kenneth H., M.D. *Kid Fitness: A Complete Shape-Up Program from Birth Through High School*. New York: Bantam Books, 1991.

Get Fit! A Handbook for Youth Ages 6-17. Washington, D.C.: President's Council on Physical Fitness and Sports, 1991.

Jacobs, Linda. *Julius Erving: Dr. J. and Julius W.* St. Paul, MN: EMC Corporation, 1976.

Kittredge, Mary. *The Human Body: An Overview*. New York: Chelsea House Publishers, 1990.

Kolata, Gina. "A Parents' Guide to Kids' Sports." *The New York Times Good Health Magazine*, April 26, 1992.

O'Neill, Catherine. "A Joint Project." *The Washington Post Health Section*, June 9, 1992.

Pantell, Robert H., M.D.; James F. Fries, M.D.; and Donald M. Vickery, M.D. *Taking Care of Your Child: A Parent's Guide to Medical Care*. Reading, MA: Addison-Wesley Publishing Co., 1984.

"Playing Fair With Young Athletes." *Taking Care,* August 1990.

"Regal Masters of Olympic Versatility," *Time,* September 19, 1988.

Schwarzenegger, Arnold. "A Secret Tragedy." *Newsweek,* May 21, 1990.

Schwarzenegger, Arnold. "Kindergarten Cop Lays Down Law on Exercise." *The New York Times,* January 6, 1991.

Vickery, Donald M., M.D. *LifePlan: Your Own Master Plan for Maintaining Health and Preventing Illness.* Reston, VA: Vicktor, Inc., 1990.

Wirhed, Rolf. *Athletic Ability: The Anatomy of Winning.* New York: Harmony Books, 1984.

Index